Tehachapi Pass

Tehachapi Pass

Poems by

David Shaddock

Cover design by Shay Culligan
Cover image by Donna Brookman

ISBN: 978-1-63980-810-6
Library of Congress Control Number: 2026932289

Kelsay Books
502 South 1040 East, A-119
American Fork, Utah 84003
Kelsaybooks.com

for Samantha, Ben, Ryan, and Ember

Acknowledgments

Poems in this collection first appeared in the journals *Star 82, Riverbabble, Brain of Forgetting (Ireland), Bosque, River Styx, Hole in the Head Review* and *Mudfish.* "Long Marriage" and "Shostakovich" appeared in the anthology *The Joy of Aging.* The Psalms in the book first appeared in *Calul.*

All props to the late John Oliver Simon for suggesting to me this hendecasyllabic, four four three three sonnet form.

The Psalms emerged from a reading of the version by Rebbe Zalman Schacter Shalomi, *Psalms in a Translation for Praying* (Aleph, 2014), as well as the translations of Robert Alter in *The Book of Psalms* (Norton, 2007). This set follows an earlier set of eighteen that were published in *Vernal Pool* (Kelsay Books, December 2014).

For advice and direction I wish to thank Peter Dale Scott, Anita Barrows, Dawn McGwire, Murray Silverstein, Carolyn Miller, Alan Williamson, Jeanne Foster, Sandra Gilbert, Phyllis Stowell, Bev Brahic, Ned Waring, and Toby Furash.

Contents

Yet stranger things I've seen of love
Who healed my wounds by wounding me.

—Giacomo da Lentini,
inventor of the sonnet

I.
Winter Light

New Year's Day

The sheen from the Bay on a Sunday is more
Catapult than surface. Our eyes make somersaults
Across the Gate from Fort Point to the Headlands
Like wind-up clowns shaken free from the toy box.

Chagall-figure clouds stretch out across the sky:
An astonished horse with his buggy above
A stretched-chimney shack where the boogeyman
Boogies. How did they all know I'd be walking

With you today on New Year's, down by the bay
Where the watermelons grow? I saw a fly
Wearing a tie I swear belonged to my father.

It's 2023 my love, one more pin knocked over by some
Pendulum, and why not, I'm thinking, Astaire
And Rogers our way down the windblown seawall?

Tehachapi Pass

Pick the lock, blow the surveillance cameras
Straight to hell, it's spring, spring, spring! with its jewels
And drool and worlds within worlds popping open
Like popcorn. Do you remember the poppies

We saw one year topping Tehachapi Pass,
The desert floor alive with orange and light-
Sparkling flecks of quartz or pyrite in the sand?
That was near Keen, where Cesar Chavez and the

UFW were headquartered. We thought there would
Be justice soon, we thought all could have what they
Need, that all could come through the needle's fine eye

And flourish again, like the barrel cactus
Flowers or the swaying stands of pampas grass—
Miles' "So What?" and distant lights of Mojave.

Raindrop

Heavy rain, then clearing. I lean over our
Neighbor's fence to admire his just-budding plum.
A clear pendant drops from each new nub, mirror
Image of the tiny bud above, emerging

From its sheath, inverted, hermetic as if
A parallel perfect world was fact, was here
All along, each singular drop a universe
Blake saw, a heaven in its downward facing

Lucent globe-enclosed plum bud. And what about
My feet on the sidewalk, whiffs of sunlit mist
Rising, shadows on the yellow stucco wall?

Shouldn't there be a blessing just for the rare times
I find myself not wishing to be elsewhere
The breeze playing each drop like a xylophone?

Vita Nuova

I’m watching the way the rain arranges
Itself, first wind and bluster, now tentative
As if waiting in line at customs. Here then
It says, gathering on the branches, car roofs

And sidewalks, settling on an insistence
It likes to pretend was there all along.
We met, years ago, on a rainy night like
This. Our talk, nothing fancy, went on and on

As if with its own momentum. We’d stop to kiss
Or gaze at the first light out the window.
We didn’t know yet that here was a *something*

The start of the life we would go on to live.
I watch your eyelids flutter as you dream.
The slow rain beats a tattoo on the skylight.

Turquoise

One minute you're about to kiss your best friend's
Ex-girlfriend, next you're barefoot on the icy
Lawn trying to get the dog to pee. Pleasure
And pain circle each other like twin Sumos.

Can we choose? There's a conference on *The New*
Science of Happiness out in Richmond this
Weekend, where they used to feed scrapyard guard dogs
Gunpowder. Now the rotting mattresses and smashed

Dishwashers are gone, they are even planning
Bike trails. *You just change your happiness setpoint.*
Remember when I bought you a bracelet from

That junktique place by the pier? It was silver
And ghost turquoise from New Mexico. I loved
The way you turned your wrist to see it in light.

Long Marriage

My fear of heights, yours of germs, grow worse
Every year, Purell always in your purse
Surface streets to avoid the 80 flyover.
I seethe, you withdraw, I pour another one

After dinner. Our worst traits run neck and neck
Toward the finish line. But love, that long shot
Is winning! We hole up and watch Steph Curry
Nail a floater and convert the plus one

Go buy the grandson rain boots at Target.
The best part is that acceptance seems programmed
To go off in our seventies, our frailties

Nesting in each other. It's like something found
At the bottom of a drawer: eyeglass screw
Chinese fan, Chagall postcards good as new.

Winter Light

Warm enough for shorts, winter light through bedroom
Windows hits us right at the small of our backs.
A dog barks, then minutes later a car starts.
I could swear I heard the grandchildren leaving

A voicemail, but there was nothing when I checked.
I'm halfway through the Sunday *Times* on global
Warming drowning Miami. Sinatra at
A hundred. I thought for many years you might

Still leave me, just as you thought that my anger
Was truer than love. As if despite ourselves
We've stumbled into grace, where a lifetime of

Mistakes can be reversed without effort.
Drowsing here in the solstice-low sunlight—
The minister of pain just left empty-handed.

Shostakovich

Liver spots on both your hands, the rings barely
Stay on your fingers. KDFC after
Dinner, something fragile but complex, turns out
It's a Shostakovich quartet. An email

This morning from Jack Foley, Jon Simon died.
He gave me this eleven syllable line
Sonnet form. I loved him, but just from afar.
I always try to manage loss by keeping

My distance. But not any longer from you
My love. You have grown as thin as your mother.
It seemed toward the end that any strong breeze

Could blow her down. But you're much stronger, outwalk
Me, eat right, follow up things with the doctor.
The cello, almost human, takes up the theme.

Three Variations on Sappho's 31st Fragment

He seems to me equal to the gods that man
—tr. Anne Carson

1.

They say it is noble to die for love
But even the lowly pond reed carries itself
With more dignity than me, telling the few
Friends who inquire I burn with infection when

I shake with wanting to smell your hair
Or brush past your wrist. All because when he stood
Near you with that sickening confidence
You didn't go inside yourself as you do

So often with me. Slim fuel for the fire
But I burn efficiently. Cold in the flame
Vitality wavers. Perhaps it's better

To die in this field than to have you see me—
Who risked everything for love—end up a
Bare twig by the roadside, trembling in the breeze.

2.

Mustard blooming in the swales and vineyards
January lambs steadier on their feet
Dry creek beds beginning to flow, milking ewes
Shorn, the wool carded, the olive trees leafed out

Starting to bud. Thunderheads on the mountain
Only light rain here. Bright hummingbirds dart
At the feeder, bonfires at night to burn off
The pruning slash, coots and grebes in standing water.

Everything lush, sedge, fern and cattail, wading
Herons and blue-winged dragonflies, spring peepers
and bullfrogs at noontime, whole clouds of

Redwinged blackbirds. Only I stand here apart
Thinking of you with him last night, unable
To speak, my insides dry as October leaves.

3.

This one sang lead in the Zeffirelli movie
Of Romeo and Juliet, that one knew
Kabbalah and rode a Triumph TR 7
And another taught poetry at San Quentin.

They all wanted you, and I still do, only
Quietly, and without hope, as if it were
A form of service. Those others are like gods
With their tongues weaving the apricot light of

Sunrise into a versified love bid.
And what they cannot get by persuasion
They take with force, their white swan wings all flapping.

I don’t want to end up some wraith in a cotton
Shift, hair down, barefoot, wandering through town
Mumbling to myself, but that’s where I’m headed.

II.
Gravity Waves

Downspout

A house is graced to have downspouts that drain rain
Far away from the foundation and gladly
Gurgle as they work, their white sides chock full of
Gutter-gathered runoff from the composite

Roof shingles, flush in their bellies like old counts
Come here for the village feast. I've run hose
Off the front ones and miss their happy noises
But the backyard is alive with freshet sound

Especially the spouts that plop on the red
Brick patio. I'm a happy guy in here—
Typing, not fighting a flood up the floorboards.

John Cipollina, that's the name that escaped me.
Quicksilver Messenger Service, Winterland.
Long flowing solos that went on forever.

Swimming Pool

One thing I like about aging is shedding
Old opinions. Who wants to swim where there's current
And muck, for instance. Pools are a jewel
Of the postwar project to improve all things.

This one in the desert is shaped like an eight
And big as a baseball diamond. Filters
So powerful they audibly whoosh. Of course
Hockney informs my seeing, but also my

Childhood days splashing at the rec center. Don't
Give me Limantour and 52 degrees.
Remember the sand fleas of Bimini, how

We itched returning on the wobbly sea plane?
Bands of blue shadow across the bottom.
Knausgaard's *My Struggle* unopened on the chaise.

Sidewalk

Roof to centipedes, roly-polies, moles, voles,
And earthworms. The city came by to grind flat
The bumps and crack-edges. After their racket
Subsided the pebbles in the aggregate

Shone like gemstones. Where to today? asks sidewalk
Sad in the drizzle. Just the curb, I'm sorry
But I have to go visit my money, which
Was my grandpa's joke for going to the bank.

Once two of your squares got tilted up like
An A-frame, but the soils guy said it's normal—
Chisel an inch off both sides and let them drop.

Tomorrow my friend I promise I'm going
To clear the decks for a trek on you, maybe
Wear flip flops in the rain. We'll go anywhere.

Yew Tree

The tip of our ornamental yew tree is
Sometimes topped by two crows who apparently
Love to sway in the wind and early morning
Fog as if on the prow of a privateer.

From late spring to early fall the green needles
Are laced through by shameless bougainvillea fronds
Reddish pink, a parasitic relation
That has evolved, at least visually, to

Symbiosis, the frankly sexual buds
Dangling around the old tree's branches. Winter
The spiky dowager arms show, her sharp thorns

Daring you to cross her. Crows come anyway
Cawing at our springer out doing her business
As the sun tries an end run past the cloudbank.

Touchless Car Wash

I sit on rickety chairs of the gravel
Waiting area with two local cops
A young Berkeley student on her smart phone
And someone my age with a small Havanese

Puppy on her lap. The sun is just burning
Off the haze and the Jettas and Camrys gleam
As the guys from Salvador and Honduras
Vacuum the insides and hand-dry the windshields.

My old Subaru comes dripping round the corner
Seeming I think a bit shy to be caught wet
In public. How my mother would have loved this.

She and Dorothy kept their new cars nice. Two
Black-and-whites, foam streaming off the siren bars
Floormats flying, chamois snapping on whitewalls.

On the Mokelumne River

Islands in the San Joaquin Delta are just swaths
Of below-sea-level farmland cut all through
By man-made sloughs, the levees dredged and stoned up
By Chinese laborers a century ago.

No palms or plumeria, fields of sorghum
And silage corn, edged round with bright sunflowers.
The chug of siphons, putput of the few bass
Trollers or Vietnamese crawdad fishermen.

Ever since 1974, when I bought
My first, a twenty-six-foot hard chined kit-built
Sloop I called Betelgeuse, I've run up here

From the Bay on the strong offshore breeze
Each time forgetting the slog to come beating
Home. Hot sun, books, a dive into the river.

On a Bench in Tilden

Cold and clear, the low parallel sun packs
A surprising punch. A flowering shrub is
A hub of busy. Two brown hummingbirds working
From branch to branch, even the tiniest twig

Unmoved by their visit. Every minute
Or so a crown of backlit white midges grows
Above the branches. I thought at first they were
Bits of duff, but they moved without any wind.

The way they rise up in waves, not random
Means they are just hatching, programmed to go off
When the day hits sixty. A pair of linnets

Descend through the insect cloud but are only
After the buckwheat. I'd been telling my friend
Some problem, but then we just sit in silence.

Gravity Waves

Late at night I click on the *Times* link and there's
One little upchirp against the background roar.
"We can hear the universe" the scientist
Says at the press conference, "from a billion

Years ago," spreading news ahead that space-time
Was deflected. Published ripples, town criers
As from Caesar or my mother reaching through
Her bad back to lift me out of the bath.

A cosmic record of two black holes passing near.
But why not me reading my son Goodnight Moon
Or Jake now to his own son, goodnight noises

Everywhere. Too small for our instruments
But here they are, unseen, passing right through us.
Goodnight dear future, boat rising up ahead.

Mr. Potato Head

I thought of myself becoming orange and round
Like the toy, just a base for anatomic
Misadventure, mustache in my naval
Feet sticking out where my ears used to be.

It seems I'm returning to the akimbo
I came from, a grin protruding from the top
Of my head like a volunteer redwood.
Hello Mabel says the mouth in my naval

though I don't know Mabel or her big sister
Evelyn. It started when my grandson moved
To the country, leaving his toys in the spare

Bedroom. They've become Pixar-noir, shelves lined with
Gaunt-face stuffed giraffes, discarded unicorns
Like Styx rowers, all pulling in unison.

Wild Thing

You're looking for a missing piece of yourself.
You're convinced it's right here in the garage
Past the boys' soccer trophies, the ones they give
Out win or lose, the baseballs all the kids sign.

Now it's after eleven and you've had
A few. Whatever happened to that old ab
Roller, the cd rom with financial
Advice, the bamboo fly rod with twice the whip

Of fiberglass? It takes a self to help your
Self, of course, that's the problem, just as it takes
Money to make money. Not even Goodwill

Will take the World Book, the flat-tired BMX.
Max wore his wolf suit. Maybe the library
Would take that—him waving so long from the boat.

III.
Extinctions

Goldilocks Planet

"Of course I have a mouth, I look a lot like
You," I say to my new-found exoplanet
Friend near Proxima Centauri. Turns out
We both breathe Oxygen. We keep it quite short

Counting our syllables, and then it does take
Eight plus years to get a reply, four each way.
"I wish I knew why we're carbonizing our air"
Was the last thing I sent him, "ruining our this-

One's-just-right planet." "Maybe you can build seawalls"
He writes back, "and at least save San Francisco."
Must be his imaging is superior.

"You don't know what you've got till it's gone" I thought
I'd tell him next time, quoting Joni Mitchell.
I dream of quartz sparkle, high desert, canteens.

Extinctions

Two out of every five pollinators
Honeybees, hummingbirds, butterflies, facing
Extinction, says Ned on the phone—I'd called for
Hoops talk. *Maybe we've just lived too long,* he says

Meaning who wants to endure the coming
Ecodystopia? Not me. Remember how
We used to hitch from Berkeley to the Haight
With strangers we called brothers, the city a peeled-

Back palimpsest of sacred texts, revealing
We thought the secret source of the world's kindness?
Almost gone now, like the sei whale or rhino.

Maybe we will leave no good record, our
Consciousness surging up and receding—
This short time here just a breach in the seawall.

Numbed

I don’t want my info dumbed down, or do I?
Would I be happier barely looking up
From a cold one at a beachside palapa
While the strongman drives by in his flagged Mercedes?

Are there any Madrids left to die for?
Where are the Marios, Stokelys, Angelas?
Apathy is outpacing empathy
Says the *Times*, and the gap is getting larger.

If you are out changing a tire in winter
Or scraping ice off driveways with a shovel
Numbness travels up the extremities.

But this, like rot, starts on the inside.
Before you know it you’re a snowman
With a carrot nose and two creekstone eyes.

Escape Plan

I've been reading up on climate change—it's all
Much closer than we could have guessed—maybe eight
Good years left us. I'm going to quit without
Waiting for my pension, move to Canada

Where research tells me I'll be safer. My wife
Can come if she wants, but she's putting the kids
In danger to stay here by the coast. Mika's
Friend from work tried to talk sense into me.

Couldn't I get a new Tesla, have an affair,
Or take up golf? They both think I've joined
Some cult I found on the Internet. North of

Winnipeg you can buy land for a song, grow
Pot as things warm up and it becomes legal.
I'll stock the cabin with classics. Are you in?

Smoke

Route 88 south of Lodi looks like Mars.
You can't see the bathroom from the gas pump.
Light through orange haze says maybe I'll kill you
Maybe I won't. Dismay, the Bay's no better.

Pittsburgh Bart, broad daylight brake lights like burning
Charcoal. No breeze through the tunnel, the City
Skeletal, everyone gasping for air like
A bad George Romero movie. Worse, the thought

That this is normal going forward, AQI
On everyone's lips, Purple Air app on smartphones—
Constant haze around Tahoe, where the kids live.

Next day at noon, total smoke-eclipse, songbirds
Roosting, darkness-sensor streetlights coming on.
Try a shower, but the dirt's on the inside.

Dia de Los Muertos

Halloween at the farmer's market, grownups
All in masks for both smoke and Covid. Ryan
Came as Marshall, the helpful fire dog from Paw
Patrol. Last year you could hold tarantulas

Or pet a python; this year the smoke is a scrim
turning the whole scene into a shadow play.
The masks have yellow straps and small plastic
filters that protrude like truncated fungi.

Why do they have the same costumes? Ryan asks.
Our friend Barbara has a Day of the Dead
Altar next to her taco truck. Faded pictures

Of her family from Mexico City
Scarves and beads, a child's mirror with a mended
Blue handle. *How did she die?* Ryan wonders.

The Future

This now is the future we've been fearing.
Floods and droughts and random violence, displaced
Persons turned back by the boatload, rallies
In the commons full of angry images

Of false nostalgia. Yeats' gyres turning
The end of a thousand-year arc from Magna
Carta to the Universal Declaration
Of the Rights of Man. Bomb-vested boys blown up

To serve the vague but voracious collective.
It reminds me of Denise's stories: huddling
In dank Blitz bomb shelters, then, nineteen, going

Out to tend the wounded. My grandson Ryan
Puts his hand in my hand as we cross toward
The schoolyard playground, his trust my antidote.

Laundry

If you stay up late reading the *Times* online
You'll know the relief a laundry basket full
Of warm-from-the-dryer t-shirts and sweatpants
Can be as you tilt and dump it out on the bed

For folding. You tuck the white drawstring
Behind the waistband, move the blue half-length arms
Of the '04 Kerry campaign shirt you now
Wear for jogging. He just spoke sternly to his

Russian counterpart over their weaponized
Hacking. The shirts crackle with static. Was Christ
The last thing on the French Priest's

Mind after the Isis guys stabbed him during
Mass, the blood soaking his cassock? Don't go there.
One sock missing, maybe in the load still drying.

Happy

Cramped in a hog hauling eighteen-wheeler off
99 near Clovis, are the pigs thinking
Whatever's next can't be worse than 102
Degrees and your butt in my face? *One must try*

Camus wrote, *to imagine Sisyphus as*
happy. I don't think he means leaping, like my
Late friend Todd, off Manawaiopuna Falls
Or tadpole *n,* ignoring their less than five

In a thousand survival rate to wriggle
Around with the rest of them. What if the ramp
Stalled in mid-air, pigs poised above the stockyard

A stick in the sprocket as if by Divine?
You have maybe fifty good poems left, said
A figure in my dream. In their bristles a breeze.

IV.
Portrait of the Artist

Symphony

I'm listening to Tchaikovsky's *Pathétique*
As the morning commute merges from the Ten
To the slow 405 near Culver City
With Herbert Von Karajan and the Berlin

Philharmonic. There's a bit of static on
KUSC which I'm fiddling to fix, so
That dates the memory to before presets.
Maybe I'm forty, still starting out but late

For something, forcing my way over for
Allenford. The woodwinds talk to violas
Whispering—Mom still alive? Not sure. The sad

Music says no. It's weird not to place yourself
In the past, no context no agency no
Self really. Last sad notes. Still true for me now?

Portrait of the Artist

These days I'm like a bed where the sheets have shrunk
The comforter leaks feathers, the box springs are
Popping through the ticking. My mother would know
A Yiddish word for me, *vertumult* or something.

I can't figure out the future: Are we doomed
Or am I depressed? The past either: is it
True that RFK was shot on June 5
1968, my twentieth birthday—

Sirhan Sirhan tackled on the seventeen-inch
Black and white? Let's not forget the present—
I'm counting these eleven syllables, one

For each finger, one more for my nose, hoping
To call sleep's angels, like birds to a feeder
To bless my poems and brush kiss these eyelids.

Worry: The Opera

We often miss the songs our worry sings
The basso profundo aria on some
Imagined armpit lump, the hope and despair
Recitative on the perils of driving

Near morons. The black ferry starts to move
Relatives scurrying down the gangplank
And waving us sadly off from the causeway.
The chorus laments us across the river

And the tenor in our belly steps forward
To throw his tiny head back and answer them.
Our taut nerves, plucked in accompaniment

Yield notes of a surprising brilliance, even
Here in Emeryville, with the wipers like batons
Conducting the suddenly tragic brake lights.

Calculus with Analytic Geometry

I can't be the only one who has this much
Trouble throwing books away. The good karma
Of library sales or the cute birdhouses
For books people put by their sidewalks are no

Help whatsoever. It's my fate, not the book's
That gets me. Every book's potential
Exit starts a little "you should have" story
Going in my head, in counterpoint with "now

You'll never." This one reminds me of the day
I walked up the stairs in Wheeler Hall to switch
Majors from math to English. I told myself

I'd fallen in love with Blake, not that I'd just
Crapped the final. Each spine a door unopened: *Surfing*
In Maui . . . A New Approach to Biblical Hebrew.

Stress Echo

The young technician with a Barbadian
Accent wants a few more strides on the treadmill
Before I can lie down for the gel and wand.
The room fills with thumps and surprising whooshes.

That's the real time rush of my own blood shooting
Out my ventricles like greyhounds. *You go, you*
Go, I'm thinking, cheering the ghostlike pictures
On the monitor. I'm looking for the news

In the tech's expression, but I bet she smiles
Like that for everybody as she rubs off
My chest with Kleenex. She's *sending on my data.*

I promise I'll stop drinking and become a vegan
I want to tell her as she closes my screen
But it's all up to the algorithm now.

In the E.R.

They're waiting for her labs. I've got a feeling
It's all good he says, squeezing her hand. *That's just*
What I hate about you, she's thinking. Neon
Light sticks to the walls like paste. The all-news crawl

About another drone strike in Yemen casts
Shadows on the beige furniture. Finally
They are called back to a room. It's not a stroke
Maybe a migraine. Does he crow just a smidgen

Does she imperceptibly recoil? She wants
None of his hand on her elbow as they
Head toward the pharmacy. I like the way

She ties her hair back with a scrunchy and wears
Hoop earrings. Is that a gold band on her finger?
Her Tramadol is ready at the window.

At the Cheeseboard

Years ago I was with my friend Robbie in
Linden, New Jersey. He'd spent ten years living
In India and was working at his dad's
Crematorium. *Death doesn't frighten me*

Anymore, he told me as we looked at blue
Gas flames coming out each of the eye sockets
Mouth and nostrils. Behind was a long tube of
Uninterrupted yellow flame consuming

The body. M. Santos said the card below
The control knobs. Robbie shrugged to say *that's all*
I know. This came back, as memories do now

From who knows where. Sun shining through coffee steam
Moms passing muffin bits down to the stroller.
6:30, give or take, I'm texting Toby.

Labile

Lately I have been crying at everything.
The skill of the backhoe guy excavating
our broken sewer line, a gesture my wife makes
that reminds me of her mother, the TV ad

where a father shaves his head to resemble
his chemo-bald son: hello human kindness
the tag line. Is this Diamond Sutra insight
The wisdom teaching of Ecclesiastes

Or a message that I need a vacation?
Labile, from the New Latin *Labi,* to fall
a term I've put on patient's insurance forms

for years. Families with graduation balloons
headed for the Greek Theater. My grandfather
Moishe, we called him Mike, got like this.

Delightful

I'm not done being delightful to someone
I wanted to tell the death that came to me
In the desert last night, but of course you can't
Move your tongue in dreams. The succulents had red

Flowers like lips, all bawdy and horrible.
Somehow it seemed important to want them all
To want me while I dodged their tendrils, though I
Never could figure out why. This dangerous

Sense of being delicious comes on early—
Right after rage and hunger. Your dimples
Blue-gray eyes, the syllabic boxes you make

As a hobby: hold them up like decoys when
Your heart goes akimbo and you fear you've bought
The farm. Be cute and your mother won't eat you.

The Depressive Position

All loving is accompanied by a death
Melanie Klein wrote. The lover, once your
Savior, bites the dust to make room for some new
Vagabond impostor. Grieve and live she meant.

The toast will never again be just the way
You like it and you are free to make a mess
Of things on your own. So of course you cry all
Through the first session with Dr. Roseblatt who makes

You reach for your own Kleenex. Nowadays we
Call it confrontation with alterity
Necessary lest you let your mom strangle

You in your sleep with a pillow. Here's
The world this morning with its clanging garbage
Trucks. It will do you good to go and greet it.

Fog

Coastal fog recalibrates the horizon
To a nearby tree or roofline instead of
The sea with its portent of greatness or loom
Of oblivion. It offers only this local

Shiver, the head bowed, the hands tucked in pockets.
In this it resembles depression in which
The sufferer is circumscribed by a problem
And the world outside is reduced to a rumor.

But this is more the inside of an iris
White splashed with pink like exuberant abstracts.
These are your own two hands, the trace of your breath

Deflected down your neck toward the sternum.
You hear surf, see scraps of cypress. You are held
By their presence, and feel that you can live now.

Coming Back from Chana's Memorial

We're dropping off Rose, leftist, eighty, who shouts
Nonsense! when Anita says she's praying for
Chana's soul each morning as she walks her dogs.
Of course it's nonsense I tell her, we need reason

More than ever. She seems unsure which is her
Stoop as we stop by her building, but declines
Our offer to walk her in. She taught with Chana
For years at Mills, but I'm not sure how close they were.

Do I still have a head? Chana, dying, asked
Her son. She meant her wits, joking to the end
He told us through tears at her memorial.

The intersection of self and door, she wrote
More than once I've walked past it. Meaning faith—
Faint light from the jamb, voices she can't quite place?

Dante on Loss: Two Poems

i. Other's Stairs

How hard a path it is for one who goes
Descending and ascending others' stairs
—Paradiso, Canto XVII, tr. Allen Mandelbaum

Strange smells in the dark hallway, the exile's trudge
Down the stairs, sudden light from outside as
The heavy door opens. But it's Ravenna
Not Florence, twelve years. The bread here too salty.

Poltava, Winnipeg, Boyle Heights, south L.A.
My own family knew exile as well.
Uncle Dave who smelled funny and wore fur hats
In summer, Wolfbear Spivak who fled the Czar's

Army and got the whole family to Winnipeg.
Strange how exile moves through my staid life
L.A. to Berkeley, one move in fifty years.

Whose green mezuzah is that on the lintel?
Whose old coats thrown over the iron banister?
It seems I've died, and other people live here.

ii. Beatrice Addresses Dante from the Chariot

I was thinking of having someone call out
My name in a poem the way Beatrice
Does to Dante in Canto XXX of Il
Purgatorio, telling him *Dante, don't*

Weep for lost Virgil, who he'd just turned to *like*
A child to his mother. So I thought it should
Be my mother, calling from Dorothy's new
Impala, *I know I'm dead but you seem down*

And we're going to lunch at May Company.
The first of a string of kind but impatient
Women who've tried to woo me from my habit

Of loneliness—Denise with her fierce English
Voice or Toby these forty years. But it's Mom
In her slippers, *I saw your light on, David.*

My Sonnets

for D.L.

Here I am contorting the speed of my thoughts
Into eleven syllables and breaking
The lines as if the right margin were some sort
Of seawall, protecting the contents from the

Slosh and slap of the Whitman free verse briny.
I'm talking as always to the ghost of Denise
Telling her of the plus one rhythm that springs
The lines free of pentameter, how I learned

It from Jon Simon, but that's what hooked, not kept
Me. They're a small room, like mine on Chautauqua
Where I could dream and read books with a flashlight

A hedged bet against the *Great Unknowing* death
Brings us up against, like kneeling, as you did
By the corner altar in your living room.

V.
Twelve Psalms

1: After Psalm 10

Forget not the Humble

How backwards everything seems, mendacity
Lauded, despoilers uplifted, the game rigged
For the rich who plump their offshore accounts while
Poor people split half a heart pill to get by.

My faith's a whisper next to the roar of despair.
You're light years away, gazing at your dazzling fan
Of galaxies. At least my oppressors know
I exist. Some days I feel like joining them.

It's a cry you want: arise YaH and go smite
The wicked. Cradle the poor, comfort orphans—
Half the time I feel like I am alone here

Talking to myself. But that's a worse dead end
Than faith. Do something about the world YaH. Don't
Sit on high and let us work it out. We won't.

2: After Psalm 28

Be not silent to me

Just outside Jaffa Gate in old Jerusalem
On the bridge that arches to Mamillia
Mall, a trumpet busker plays Strangers in the
Night to the thump of a prerecorded track.

Even as you are everywhere, YaH, I often feel
That I am nowhere at all, like someone just
Released from a long confinement. What am I
But a splash of discordant urges, ready

To flee or to fight by rote for something I've
Long forgotten. I envy the fringed Frum for
Their apparent certainty, but here I am

Still gyrating between praise and doubt like a
Frictionless piston. Be my *strength and shield*, Yah
Let my heart rejoice as the old song promised.

3: After Psalm 29

The Lord Shaketh the Wilderness

Great thunder wakes me, then rain on the tile roof.
I open my glass door to see the whole crest
Of the Sangre de Christos lit up by forked
Lightning. New Mexico, Jerusalem, all

The places where you bellow from high like a
Mountain ram or scree like a red tail hawk. I'm
Barefoot, in bed clothes, curled back under the eaves
Trying to let my body respond to this.

You're no good to us far away YaH, it's here
Where we need you, the sage and prickly cactus
The cows in the metal roofed barn, my feet my

Hips the top of my diaphragm. Ponderosa
Pine and incense cedar, the slight ozone smell
After lightning, the wet musk of the forest floor.

4: After Psalm 34

O Taste and See that the Lord is Good.

Here's the metallic chemotherapy
Aftertaste, the salty blood in the mouth that
Is your first hint you are not okay after
The car crash, the moldy rind, poison mushroom

Unshakable bile. Did you see the Angel
As you lay there, with half your eyes, half your mind
Sprinkling the joins with gold, matching the patterns
Of the rent. O taste now and see how the Lord

Is good, that every breath is a knitting
Of this world to the next. The dying
Can taste this, beneath the Mercury the lead

The loam. I sought YaH and he did answer me.
Not precisely sweetness, but something acid
Turns to, attar of rosemary, tangerines.

5: After Psalm 39

Behold thou hast made my days as a handbreadth

I have a different hope for myself, YaH.
I don't want my soul to leak out like old wine
from a loose-staved barrel or be sold like junk
from an unpaid storage unit. I know I've

Joined in gossip, felt the pleasure of directing
Scorn at others, away from myself. Mother's
Love, your presence on earth, I spurned it until
It was too late and she was gone. All along

I had glimpses, Kol Nidre, all vows renounced
All promises renewed. Times when songs of praise
Rolled off my tongue unbidden. Don't tell me we're

All one piece, that good and evil mingle. I've
Glimpsed the figured wheel, the stone path curving up
The viewpoint. I need to know that there's still time.

6: After Psalm 40

He brought me up also out of a horrible pit

For days I felt like I was in some clever
Cage. It's microns-thin but impenetrable
Walls moved when I moved, contoured to my breathing.
Clear, I saw the world go on, the 65

Bus stop at the corner, the middle school kids
Get off and run toward their houses. No one
Saw me, no emails, texts, or instant message.
If I flailed the walls expanded, I collapsed

And they shrunk to meet me. *Help me YaH*, I cried
But I was convinced that you could not hear me.
Then I woke and the world was with me again

Tremulous as a fledgling. God will prevail,
The old text reads and why not believe it, bless
Me, *lowly and needy,* pavement, weather, breath.

7: After Psalm 41

Blessed is he that considereth the poor

Care for the poor and you will become happy.
Ignore them and your enemies will crawl out
Of the woodwork like termites sharpening their
Mandibles. Do good and all those who want you

Dead will be disappointed. All the fungi
Will pause from eating your mitral valve lining
If you give alms or work to revive Nixon's
Guaranteed annual income. Do this and

The early and late rains will come. Let homeless
Camp squalor line every riverside and
The fertile valleys will lie scorched the sea will

Rise and swallow Manhattan. The viruses
Are mutating. Do you want to keep thinking
The poor somehow deserve their scabs and breadcrusts?

8: After Psalm 42

As the hart panteth after the water brooks

My heart a stag, running ahead, leaping fences
Dancing over hedgerows, across the meadow
Into the cottonwoods, out toward the stream
Crashing down the bank gravel then dipping

A graceful long neck to drink, drops of water
Glistening from the many pointed antlers.
Once in a while, YaH, you let me out from my
Body, from my one life into the many.

My enemies haven't disappeared, they tap
My phone, intercept my text, match me up with
Their lists. But they can't find me here, in the copse

Become ouzel, pied trout, water strider, stag
Or doe. They crash the brush, whistle for the dogs
But I am too still, a single syllable.

9: After Psalm 43

Upon the harp will I praise thee

I will play music at your holy mountain.
I will add my off-key alto to the choir.
I will strum a minor sixth and invoke your
Holy Name. I will blast on top of the brushed

Snare and fingered bass like Coltrane breaking through
Mid-thought into 32nd note flights of
Ecstasy, a prismed splay of water
On my glasses by the waterfall splash pool.

I will improvise on oil drum lids, tissue
Covered combs, innards of junkyard pianos
Strummed with raven feathers. With my beloved

I'll dance a slow and stately Hora. Doumbek
And oud spin us around while we ignore the fires
Of our enemies spread out beyond the river.

10: After Psalm 46

Though the mountains be carried into the midst of the sea

Everything shudders like a shot raptor. Ice
Caps groan in distress, sheets of glaciers break off
And fall to the sea with a cataclysmic
Roar. All around the Pacific Rim the faults

Ratchet up: volcanoes spew, earthquakes run cross
The tundra, Everest trembles, avalanches
Crush valley hamlets, stupas and heiaus buried
In snow or lava. No rain for decades on

The plains east of Denver, barrio Texas
Bordertowns flooded by the swollen Brazos
Or high brown Rio Grande. I do not need

To be convinced of your power, YaH, but of
Your mercy I am less certain. Would you spare
Us for ten just men, for one who still fears you?

11: After Psalm 51

Cast me not away from thy presence

A broken and a contrite heart, O YaH, thou
Wilt not despise. How long I lived searching
For solutions to suffering, pouring out
My litany of slights and remorse to any

Professional listener, copying into
Lined notebooks the Diamond Sutra, taking
Herbs and acupuncture, thumb-typing your name
Into my smartphone search engine. This is the

Season of truth, of slant light and warm days laced
Through with a breeze of winter. Now the dragon
Circles the pole star, hungry loins coiled around

Darkness. What if all I am beneath my shame
Is nothing? A flash I've fended and fended.
Even then I've thought and prayed and hoped you'd love me.

12: After Psalm 51

Renew a right spirit within me

Sonnet after sonnet trying for a turn
A flip, ironic or discarding irony.
But will there, in my life, be a turn where
I reach the end of fighting and acquiring

And say, and moreover mean, *cleanse me YaH, scrub*
Me as white as snow. Be someone I've never
Known, not mother, therapist, rabbi—but pure
Transformation, merciless mercy, sore bones

Scoured hollow like a flute the wind plays. I don't
Want to be detached from the world, YaH. Make me
Into someone like Denise Levertov, for whom

Each *minim mote* of the world is a spark, like
Caedmon, in her poem, holding a lit piece
Of barn straw, then all at once called up to dance.

Notes

p. 17. *where the watermelons grow* is part of a lyric from a children's song "Down By the Bay" which also includes the line *I thought I saw a fly/wearing a tie/Down by the bay.*

p. 21. *the new science of happiness.* The conference was sponsored by The Greater Good Science Center at UC Berkeley.

p. 25. *Three Variations On Sappho's 31st Fragment.* Credit to Dawn McGuire for suggesting we try this.

p. 43. *Goldilocks Planet.* The name scientists have coined for an exoplanet (e.g. one outside the Solar System) that would seem to have the necessary chemical makeup to support life.

p. 49. *going out to tend the wounded.* Denise Levertov served in the Civil Nursing Reserve during the bombardment of London.

p. 63. *The Depressive Position.* The name (which has nothing to do with clinical depression) which Melanie Klein gave to the developmental step where the infant renounces his exclusive hold on the mother and realizes his separateness.

p. 66. *The intersection of self and door.* Chana Bloch, (1940-2017) "At the Intersection." *The Moon is Almost Full* (2017) Autumn House Press.

p. 68. *Weep for lost Virgil.* My own father, a poet, died when I was fifteen.

p. 69. *Great Unknowing.* Denise Levertov, *The Great Unknowing: Last Poems.* (New Directions, 1999).

Twelve Psalms. These are part of an ongoing project to write sonnets to the Psalms that move me. Previous ones have appeared in *Vernal Pool* and *The Book of Splendor.* The quoted passages are from Robert Alter, The Book of Psalms (Norton, 2007) or the King James Version.

p. 73 ff. *YaH.* One syllable reference to the unpronounceable name of God, popular in Jewish Renewal services.

p. 84. *Minim mote.* Denise Levertov, "Mass for the Day of St. Thomas Didymus."

About the Author

David Shaddock's poems have appeared in *Mother Jones, Tikkun, Hanging Loose,* and *EarthFirst! Journal.* He is the author of four books of poems, including *Vernal Pool* and *The Book of Splendor: New and Selected Poems on Spiritual Themes.* His work received the International Peace Poetry Prize and the Ruah Magazine prize for a collection of spiritual poems.

He is also the author of three nonfiction books, including, most recently, *Poetry and Psychoanalysis: The Opening of the Field.* His column, Poetry and Healing, appears in *Poetry Flash.* He has a psychotherapy practice in Berkeley.

www.ingramcontent.com/pod-product-compliance
Lightning Source LLC
LaVergne TN
LVHW020653100826
845148LV00012B/2461
* 9 7 8 1 6 3 9 8 0 8 1 0 6 *